T0275330

The Hound
of Heaven

The Hound *of* Heaven

Francis Thompson

WITH DECORATIONS BY
JEAN YOUNG

MOREHOUSE PUBLISHING
HARRISBURG, PA

THE HOUND OF HEAVEN

I FLED Him, down the nights and down the
    days;
  I fled Him, down the arches of the years;
I fled Him, down the labyrinthine ways
    Of my own mind; and in the mist of tears
I hid from Him, and under running laughter.
        Up vistaed hopes, I sped;
        And shot, precipitated,

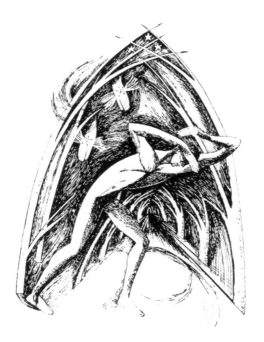

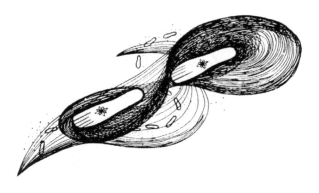

Adown Titanic glooms of chasmèd fears,
From those strong Feet that followed,
followed after.

But with unhurrying chase,
    And unperturbèd pace,
Deliberate speed, majestic instancy,
    They beat—and a Voice beat
    More instant than the Feet—
'All things betray thee, who betrayest Me.'

I PLEADED, outlaw-wise,
By many a hearted casement, curtained red,
    Trellised with intertwining charities
(For, though I knew His love Who followèd,
        Yet was I sore adread
Lest, having Him, I must have naught beside);
But, if one little casement parted wide,
    The gust of His approach would clash it to.
    Fear wist not to evade as Love wist to pursue.

ACROSS the margent of the world I fled,
　　And troubled the gold gateways of the stars,
　　Smiting for shelter on their clangèd bars;
　　　　　Fretted to dulcet jars
And silvern chatter the pale ports o' the moon.
I said to dawn: Be sudden; to eve: Be soon—
　　With thy young skyey blossoms heap me over
　　　　　From this tremendous Lover!
Float thy vague veil about me, lest He see!

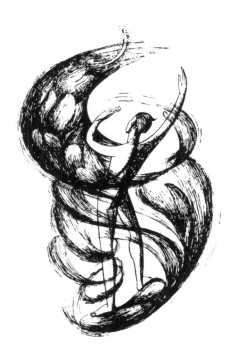

I TEMPTED all His servitors, but to find
My own betrayal in their constancy,
In faith to Him their fickleness to me,
   Their traitorous trueness, and their loyal
      deceit.
To all swift things for swiftness did I sue;
   Clung to the whistling mane of every wind.
   But whether they swept, smoothly fleet,
The long savannahs of the blue;
   Or whether, Thunder-driven,
They clanged His chariot 'thwart a heaven,
Plashy with flying lightnings round the spurn
      o' their feet:—
   Fear wist not to evade as Love wist to pursue.

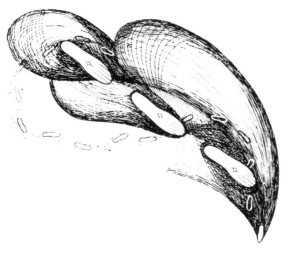

Still with unhurrying chase,
And unperturbèd pace,
Deliberate speed, majestic instancy,

Came on the following Feet,
And a Voice above their beat—
'Naught shelters thee, who wilt not shelter Me.'

I SOUGHT no more that after which I strayed
    In face of man or maid;
But still within the little children's eyes
    Seems something, something that replies,
They at least are for me, surely for me!
I turned me to them very wistfully;
But just as their young eyes grew sudden fair

With dawning answers there,
Their angel plucked them from me by the hair.

'Come then, ye other children, Nature's—
    share
With me' (said I) 'your delicate fellowship;
  Let me greet you lip to lip,
  Let me twine with you caresses,
        Wantoning
  With our Lady-Mother's vagrant tresses,
        Banqueting
  With her in her wind-walled palace,
  Underneath her azured daïs,
  Quaffing, as your taintless way is,
        From a chalice
  Lucent-weeping out of the dayspring.'
        So it was done:

I in their delicate fellowship was one—
Drew the bolt of Nature's secrecies.
    I knew all the swift importings
    On the wilful face of skies;
    I knew how the clouds arise,
    Spumèd of the wild sea-snortings;
      All that's born or dies
  Rose and drooped with; made them shapers
Of mine own moods, or wailful or divine—
    With them joyed and was bereaven.
    I was heavy with the even,
  When she lit her glimmering tapers
    Round the day's dead sanctities.

Deliberate speed, majestic instancy.

I laughed in the morning's eyes.
I triumphed and I saddened with all weather,
Heaven and I wept together,

And its sweet tears were salt with mortal mine;
Against the red throb of its sunset-heart
        I laid my own to beat,
        And share commingling heat;
But not by that, by that, was eased my human
    smart.
In vain my tears were wet on Heaven's grey
    cheek.
For ah! we know not what each other says,
      These things and I; in sound *I* speak—
Their sound is but their stir, they speak by
    silences.
Nature, poor stepdame, cannot slake my drouth;

Let her, if she would owe me,
Drop yon blue bosom-veil of sky, and show me
The breasts o' her tenderness:
Never did any milk of hers once bless
My thirsting mouth.

NIGH and nigh draws the chase,
With unperturbèd pace,
Deliberate speed, majestic instancy,
And past those noisèd Feet
A Voice comes yet more fleet—
'Lo! naught contents thee, who content'st not
Me.'

Naked I wait Thy love's uplifted stroke!
My harness piece by piece Thou hast hewn
from me,

And smitten me to my knee;
I am defenceless utterly.
I slept, methinks, and woke.
And, slowly gazing, find me stripped in sleep.
In the rash lustihead of my young powers,
I shook the pillaring hours
And pulled my life upon me; grimed with
smears,
I stand amid the dust o' the mounded years—
My mangled youth lies dead beneath the heap.
My days have crackled and gone up in smoke,
Have puffed and burst as sun-starts on a stream.

Yea, faileth now even dream
The dreamer, and the lute the lutanist;
Even the linked fantasies, in whose blossomy
    twist
I swung the earth a trinket at my wrist,
Are yielding; cords of all too weak account
For earth, with heavy griefs so overplussed.
        Ah! is Thy love indeed
A weed, albeit an amaranthine weed,
Suffering no flowers except its own to mount?
            Ah! must—
            Designer infinite!—
Ah! must Thou char the wood ere Thou canst
    limn with it?
My freshness spent its wavering shower i' the
    dust;
And now my heart is as a broken fount,
Wherein tear-drippings stagnate, spilt down
    ever
        From the dank thoughts that shiver

Upon the sighful branches of my mind.
      Such is; what is to be?
The pulp so bitter, how shall taste the rind?
I dimly guess what Time in mists confounds;
Yet ever and anon a trumpet sounds
From the hid battlements of Eternity;
Those shaken mists a space unsettle, then
Round the half-glimpsèd turrets slowly wash
    again;
      But not ere him who summoneth
      I first have seen, enwound
With glooming robes purpureal, cypress-
    crowned,
His name I know, and what his trumpet saith.
Whether man's heart or life it be which yields
      Thee harvest, must Thy harvest fields
      Be dunged with rotten death?

Now of that long pursuit
Comes on at hand the bruit;
That Voice is round me like a bursting sea:
    'And is thy earth so marred,
    Shattered in shard on shard?
Lo, all things fly thee, for thou fliest Me!
    Strange, piteous, futile thing,
Wherefore should any set thee love apart?
Seeing none but I makes much of naught' (He
    said),
'And human love needs human meriting:
    How hast thou merited—
Of all man's clotted clay the dingiest clot?

Alack, thou knowest not
How little worthy of any love thou art!
Whom wilt thou find to love ignoble thee,
    Save Me, save only Me?
All which I took from thee I did but take,
    Not for thy harms,
But just that thou might'st seek it in My arms.
    All which thy child's mistake
Fancies as lost, I have stored for thee at home:
    Rise, clasp My hand, and come.'

Rise, clasp My hand, and come.

Halts by me that footfall:
Is my gloom, after all,
Shade of His hand, outstretched caressingly?
'Ah, fondest, blindest, weakest,
I am He whom thou seekest!
Thou dravest love from thee, who dravest Me.'

First Published in Great Britian in 1947

Sixteenth U.S. impression 2008

Morehouse Publishing, 4785 Linglestown Road, Suite 101,
Harrisburg, PA 17112
Morehouse Publishing, 19 East 34th Street, New York, NY 10016

Morehouse Publishing
is an imprint of
Church Publishing Incorporated

ISBN : 978-0-8192-1205-4

Printed in the U.S.A